PORTRAITS OF THE

★ ★

VERMONT

by Jonatha A. Brown

Gareth Stevens
Publishing

Please visit our web site at: www.garethstevens.com
For a free color catalog describing Gareth Stevens Publishing's
list of high-quality books and multimedia programs, call
1-800-542-2595 (USA) or 1-800-387-3178 (Canada).
Gareth Stevens Publishing's fax: (877) 542-2596.

Library of Congress Cataloging-in-Publication Data

Brown, Jonatha A.
    Vermont / Jonatha A. Brown.
      p. cm. — (Portraits of the states)
    Includes bibliographical references and index.
    ISBN-10: 0-8368-4710-5 ISBN-13: 978-0-8368-4710-9 (lib. bdg.)
    ISBN-10: 0-8368-4727-X ISBN-13: 978-0-8368-4727-7 (softcover)
    1. Vermont—Juvenile literature. I. Title. II. Series.
  F49.3.B76   2007
  974.3—dc22   2005036642

This edition first published in 2007 by
Gareth Stevens Publishing
A Weekly Reader Company
1 Reader's Digest Rd.
Pleasantville, NY 10570-7000 USA

This edition copyright © 2007 by Gareth Stevens, Inc.

Editorial direction: Mark J. Sachner
Project manager: Jonatha A. Brown
Editor: Catherine Gardner
Art direction and design: Tammy West
Picture research: Diane Laska-Swanke
Indexer: Walter Kronenberg
Production: Jessica Morris and Robert Kraus

Picture credits: Cover, p. 20 © Tim Seaver; p. 4 © Pat & Chuck Blackley;
p. 5 © Steve Maslowski/Visuals Unlimited; pp. 6, 9 © North Wind Picture Archives;
p. 8 © Stock Montage/Getty Images; p. 10 © Joseph Sohm; ChromoSohm Inc./
CORBIS; pp. 12, 21 © Paul Rezendes/www.paulrezendes.com; pp. 15, 24, 28
© Gibson Stock Photography; pp. 16, 25 © AP Images; p. 22 © Kevin Fleming/
CORBIS; p. 26 © Phil Schermeister/CORBIS; p. 27 © James P. Rowan; p. 29
© John Elk III

Printed in the United States of America

3 4 5 6 7 8 9 10 09 08 07

CONTENTS

★ ★

Chapter 1 Introduction........................4

Chapter 2 History............................6

Time Line 13

Chapter 3 People 14

Chapter 4 The Land..........................18

Chapter 5 Economy...........................22

Chapter 6 Government 24

Chapter 7 Things to See and Do 26

Glossary 30

To Find Out More..................31

Index 32

Words that are defined in the Glossary appear
in **bold** the first time they are used in the text.

On the Cover: Fall is a beautiful time of year in Vermont! Here, the
slopes near Worcester Village are beginning to show their fall colors.

Introduction

When you think of Vermont, what comes to mind? Steep ski slopes covered with deep powder? Pretty towns and quiet country roads? Golden maple syrup? These are just a few of the things that make Vermont famous.

This state is well known as the home of Ethan Allen and his Green Mountain Boys. Long ago, Allen and his men fought for Vermont and freedom. Vermont also is one of the few U.S. states that was once a separate country, and it was the first to outlaw slavery. The people of Vermont have long stood up for themselves and looked out for others.

Today, the people of Vermont welcome guests. They look forward to sharing the beauty of their state with you.

Vermont is well known for its many charming villages.

The state flag of Vermont.

VERMONT FACTS

- Became the 14th U.S. State: March 4, 1791
- Population (2006): 623,908
- Capital: Montpelier
- Biggest Cities: Burlington, Essex, Rutland, Colchester
- Size: 9,250 square miles (23,958 square kilometers)
- Nickname: The Green Mountain State
- State Tree: Sugar maple
- State Flower: Red clover
- State Animal: Morgan horse
- State Bird: Hermit thrush

History

For at least nine thousand years, Native Americans have lived in the area that is now Vermont. At first, they hunted big animals. Later, they also caught fish and found wild plants to eat. Natives in this area began farming about one thousand years ago. These people grew squash, corn, and beans.

By the 1500s, two groups of Natives lived here. They were the Abenaki and the Iroquois. They were enemies. The two groups often fought over the land.

Early Europeans

The first European who is known to have reached Vermont was a French explorer. Samuel de Champlain came south from Canada in 1609. He reached Lake Champlain, and he saw the Green Mountains. Champlain met the Abenaki people along the way. He and his men helped them fight the Iroquois. Then, Champlain claimed this land for France.

Samuel de Champlain and a group of Abenakis attack an Iroquois village along the shores of Lake Champlain.

The French built the first European settlement here in 1666. They built it on an island in Lake Champlain. They named it Fort Sainte Anne. This settlement did not last long. The settlers soon gave up and left.

Fighting over the Land

France and Britain wanted the land in Vermont. Both of them wanted other lands on the Atlantic Coast, too. The two countries fought for control of this area for almost a **century**. During this time, even more white settlers came to Vermont.

The last war between the British and French began in 1754. This was the French and Indian War. In this war, the Abenaki sided with the French. The Iroquois sided with the British. After nine years, Britain won. Now, the British held thirteen **colonies** along the East Coast.

After the war ended, both New Hampshire and New York claimed Vermont. The two colonies argued over the land for years. Many of the Vermont settlers had bought **property** from the governor of New Hampshire. Now, New York wanted to take over and make them pay for their land again. So, most settlers wanted to keep New York from taking control.

Ethan Allen was a Revolutionary War hero. Here, Allen wakes up a British general and tells him that he has captured the general's fort!

Famous People of Vermont

Ethan Allen

Born: January 21, 1738, Litchfield, Connecticut

Died: February 12, 1789, Burlington, Vermont

Ethan Allen owned property in Vermont. He did not want New York to claim his land. In 1770, he formed a band of fighters to keep New York from taking over land in Vermont. Allen's group became known as the Green Mountain Boys. For five years, they fought with the "Yorkers." When the Revolutionary War began, Allen's group stopped fighting the Yorkers. Instead, they fought the British. Allen was captured during the war and spent two years in prison. He was a hero to many people in Vermont.

These settlers are hauling maple sap in the 1800s. They will use the sap to make sweet maple syrup.

Soon, a bigger problem came up. Many colonists had grown tired of British control. They wanted to be free. In 1775, they started to fight the Revolutionary War. Many people from Vermont joined the fight.

Becoming a State

During the war, the people of Vermont formed their own country. They called it New Connecticut. Slavery was against the law, and all men who lived there could vote, even those who did not own land. These ideas were very new at the time.

The people of Vermont wanted their country to be a U.S. state. But the leaders of New Hampshire and New York did not like this idea. They would not allow it.

The war ended in 1783. Several years later, New York and New Hampshire stopped trying to claim Vermont. In 1791, Vermont became a U.S. state.

The State Grows

Over the next twenty years, thousands of people moved to Vermont. Most of them became farmers. Others worked in small factories. They sawed lumber, wove cloth, and made other goods. Many of these products were sold to people in Canada.

In the early 1800s, the nation's first granite quarry opened in Vermont. Today, the state is home to the biggest granite quarry in the world.

IN VERMONT'S HISTORY

The War of 1812
The United States and Britain went to war again in 1812. A shipyard in Vergennes built ships that fought in this war. The last big battle of the war took place on Lake Champlain in 1814. Two ships from Vergennes beat the British that day.

The Champlain Canal was dug in the early 1820s. It linked Lake Champlain to the Hudson River in New York. The canal helped people in Vermont ship goods to New York and other states more easily. In the mid-1800s, rail lines were built through Vermont. This made shipping even easier and faster.

Trains soon brought more people to the state. Settlers came from Italy and Wales. They worked in Vermont's granite and marble **quarries**. People came from Canada and Ireland, too. They often found work in **factories** and on railroads.

Facing Change

In the late 1800s, Vermont had problems. Many people moved away to live in the West. Cloth factories left the state, too. They moved to other states where costs were lower. Some businesses did well. Granite was in great demand, so the state's quarries made money. Dairy farming grew during this period, too.

Vermont became a hot vacation spot in the early 1900s. Thousands of **tourists** came to the state each year. Hotels and camps were built for these visitors. Tourism created new jobs and brought money into the state.

Factories also began to do better. Many new factories were built. During World War I and World War II, the factory workers in Vermont made war supplies. Other people from the state served as soldiers. They helped win these two wars.

FUN FACTS

Two Presidents

Two men from Vermont have been U.S. president. In 1880, Chester A. Arthur was elected vice president. He became president the next year, after James A. Garfield was killed. Calvin Coolidge was elected vice president in 1920. When Warren G. Harding died in office, Coolidge served in his place. He then ran for another term and won. He served for five years.

IN VERMONT'S HISTORY

Civil War Battle

The Civil War was fought from 1861 to 1865. Vermont sided with the North. Soldiers from this state fought against soldiers from the southern states. No battles took place in Vermont. Still, in 1864, southern forces came to the state. They robbed banks in St. Albans and escaped to Canada with the money. Even so, they lost the war.

Farming is still a way of life for some families in Vermont.

As factories grew, farming became less popular. Many people sold their farms and moved to the cities to work.

Lovely Vermont

Since 1960, Vermont has been growing fast. Many people have moved here from nearby states. Some have left their homes in big cities and moved to peaceful places in the country.

The people of Vermont work hard to keep their state beautiful. In 1984, they set aside almost one-fourth of the state's land. This land in the Green Mountains will be kept wild forever. The state has also set limits on growth in cities. These controls help Vermont keep its charm.

Today, Vermont is known for its small farms. It has a **thriving** tourist industry, too. This state is a good place to live and work.

FUN FACTS

Keeping Vermont Beautiful

Many people in Vermont think **billboards** are ugly. They have passed laws to keep these big signs from being put up in their state. Only three other states have outlawed billboards.

★ ★ ★ Time Line ★ ★ ★

1609	Samuel de Champlain becomes the first European to visit Vermont.
1724	The British build the first lasting European settlement at Fort Dummer.
1763	Britain takes over Vermont after winning the French and Indian War.
1777	Vermont becomes the **republic** of New Connecticut.
1791	Vermont becomes a U.S. state on March 4.
1814	Ships built in Vergennes beat the British in the last big battle of the War of 1812.
1861-1865	Vermont fights on the side of the **Union** during the Civil War.
1881	Chester A. Arthur becomes U.S. president.
1917-1918	Vermont helps the United States fight in World War I.
1923	Calvin Coolidge becomes U.S. president.
1941-1945	Vermont factory workers and soldiers help fight World War II.
1984	Parts of the Green Mountain National Forest are set aside as wilderness areas.

People

More than 620,000 people live in the state of Vermont. Only one other U.S. state has a smaller **population**. More than two-thirds of the people in this state live on farms or in small towns. Vermont has almost two hundred fifty villages and small towns.

Burlington is Vermont's biggest city. Nearly 40,000 people live there. Many tourists visit this city in the summer. It is the state's center for trade, shipping, and travel, too.

Hispanics

This chart shows the different racial backgrounds of people in Vermont. In the 2000 U.S. Census, 0.9 percent of the people in Vermont called themselves Latino or Hispanic. Most of them or their relatives came from places where Spanish is spoken. Hispanics do not appear on this chart because they may come from any racial background.

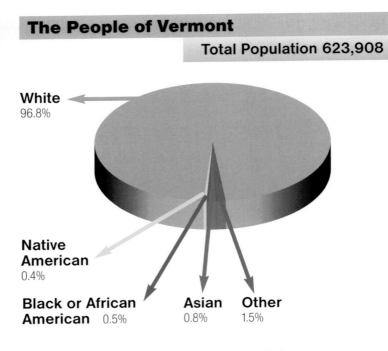

The People of Vermont

Total Population 623,908

White
96.8%

Native American
0.4%

Black or African American 0.5%

Asian 0.8%

Other 1.5%

Percentages are based on the 2000 Census.

The next largest cities in the state are Essex, Rutland, and Colchester. These three cities are less than one-half the size of Burlington. The state capital is Montpelier, but it is not very big. In fact, it is the smallest state capital in the nation. Only about 8,000 people live in Vermont's capital city.

People of the Past

The first white people to live here came from France and Britain. Later, many French-speaking people came to this area from Canada. Most of

Burlington lies on the eastern shore of Lake Champlain. Settled in the 1770s, it became the biggest city in the state.

them settled in the northern part of the state. **Immigrants** from Italy, Spain, and Wales settled near Barre so they could work in the stone quarries nearby. Settlers from Ireland and Poland came here, too. Most of them found work on the railroads and in factories.

The People Today

Today, nearly all of the people who live here are

15

In May 2006, the leaders of Vermont officially recognized the Abenakis who live here. In this picture, a group of Abenakis celebrate this important event.

white. Only about 3 percent of all the people in Vermont are of some other race. Less than 1 percent of the people are Hispanic.

Few people are moving here from other countries today. Canadians make up the largest group. Some people are coming here from India, China, and other parts of the world, too.

Religion and Education

Roman Catholics make up the largest religious group in the state. Many Methodists and Baptists also live here. Other groups in Vermont include Lutherans and Jews.

In this state, schools have been important for a long

time. The first plan for public schools was written in the late 1700s. A school for training teachers opened in Concord in 1823. It was the first school of this kind in the United States. Three years later, the state began to collect taxes to pay for the state's schools. Today, nearly nine out of every ten adults in Vermont have finished high school.

Vermont has more than twenty universities and colleges. The first was the University of Vermont. It was founded in 1791 in Burlington. Today, about ten thousand students go to school there. The state has fine private colleges, too. Middlebury and Bennington Colleges are among them. The School for International Training in Brattleboro is another.

Famous People of Vermont

Katherine Paterson

Born: October 31, 1932, Qing Jiang, China

Katherine Paterson was born in China. Her parents were **missionaries**. They wanted to teach their religion to people in other lands. Katherine and her family moved eighteen times before she was eighteen years old! When she was young, she wanted to be a movie star or a missionary. Instead, she grew up to be a famous writer. She has written many children's books. Some of them have won awards. Two of her most well-known books are *Jacob Have I Loved* and *Bridge to Terabithia*. Some of her books take place in Vermont. She lives in Barre.

The Land

Vermont is in the northeastern part of the United States. It is in an area known as **New England**. Compared to other states, Vermont is small. It ranks forty-third in land area.

Two of the state's borders are along waterways. The western border cuts through Lake Champlain. On the east, the border is formed by the Connecticut River.

Lowlands

The land near Lake Champlain is made up of low, rolling hills that are covered with rich soil. Many dairy farms and apple orchards can be seen here. The state's largest city, Burlington, is in this part of Vermont, as well.

Another low area in the west is the Vermont Valley. This narrow valley lies between the Taconic and Green Mountains. A third lowland area is known as the New England Uplands. This region lies along the Connecticut River. Its rolling hills are lowest near the river. The hills grow higher as they near the mountains.

VERMONT

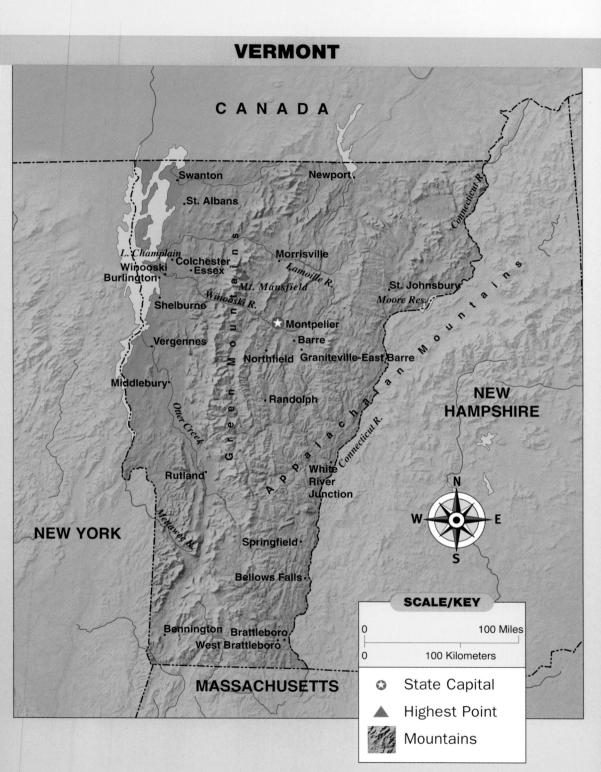

CANADA

Swanton

Newport

St. Albans

L. Champlain

Morrisville

Lamoille R.

Colchester
Essex

Winooski
Burlington

Mt. Mansfield

Winooski R.

St. Johnsbury

Moore Res.

Shelburne

Montpelier

Barre

Vergennes

Northfield

Graniteville-East Barre

Middlebury

Randolph

Green Mountains

Otter Creek

Appalachian Mountains

Connecticut R.

Connecticut R.

NEW
HAMPSHIRE

Rutland

White
River
Junction

N

W   E

S

NEW YORK

Metawee R.

Springfield

Bellows Falls

Bennington

Brattleboro
West Brattleboro

MASSACHUSETTS

SCALE/KEY

0	100 Miles
0	100 Kilometers

⊛ State Capital

▲ Highest Point

▨ Mountains

19

Mountains

Mountains cover the rest of Vermont. Running through the center of the state from north to south are the Green Mountains. They are part of the Appalachian Mountains, which run along much of the East Coast. Mount Mansfield is in the Green Mountains. It is the highest point in the state. Mount Mansfield stands 4,393 feet (1,339 meters) high.

The Taconic Mountains are in the southwestern part of the state. Big marble deposits are found here. Another area of mountains is in the northeast. It is the Northeast Highlands. The land in the Highlands is mostly made up of a hard rock called granite.

Major Rivers

Connecticut River
407 miles (655 km) long

Otter Creek
100 miles (160 km) long

Winooski River
100 miles (160 km) long

Waterways

The longest river in the state is the Connecticut River. Most of the streams on the east side of the mountains flow into this river.

The peaks of Mount Mansfield are reflected in the quiet waters of a mountain pond.

FUN FACTS

Brrrrrr!

Vermont has long, cold, snowy winters and short summers. Summer days are warm, but the air grows cool in the evenings. Some of the mountains have snow on their peaks all year long.

The state has at least eight hundred lakes and ponds. The largest is Lake Champlain. Most rivers on the western side of the mountains flow into this lake.

Plants and Animals

More than 75 percent of the land here is covered with forests. Oak, elm, maple, and birch trees are common. The sugar maple is the state tree. Its leaves turn bright yellow, orange, and red in the fall.

Pines and firs grow in the mountains. Wildflowers such as violets, daisies, and goldenrod grow in Vermont.

In the higher parts of the mountains live moose, bears, and bobcats. Large numbers of white-tailed deer live in the state. Vermont's smaller animals include coyotes, beavers, otters, foxes, mink, and porcupines.

The Connecticut River forms the western border of the state. It is the longest river in Vermont.

Economy

Today, farming is not as important in Vermont as it once was. Even so, almost one-fourth of the land in the state is used for farming. Vermont has about six thousand farms. Most of them are dairy farms. Almost half of the milk in New England comes from Vermont. Other farms in the state are used to raise chickens for eggs. Still others are used to grow hay, fruits, vegetables, and Christmas trees. Vermont is also the top producer of maple syrup in the country.

Making Goods and Mining

For the past one hundred years, factories have brought more money into the state

Some farmers near St. Albans still use horses and sleds to collect sap for making maple sugar and syrup.

than farms. Today, some factories make computer parts. Others make guns and tools for working with metal. Still others print books and newspapers. Factories in Vermont also make milk products. They include ice cream, cheese, butter, and yogurt.

Vermont is still a big producer of granite. This hard rock is used in many buildings. High-quality marble is mined in the state, too.

Tourism

Tourism provides jobs for many people who live in this state. These jobs are in restaurants, ski **resorts**, hotels, and other places tourists like to go. The most important tourist industry here is skiing.

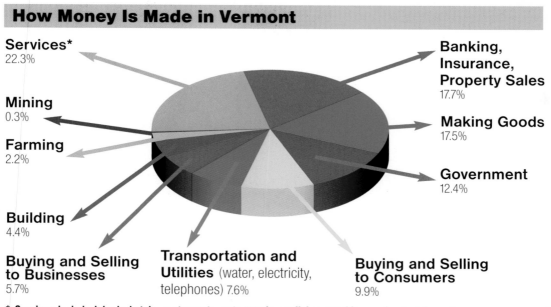

How Money Is Made in Vermont

Services*
22.3%

Mining
0.3%

Farming
2.2%

Building
4.4%

Banking, Insurance, Property Sales
17.7%

Making Goods
17.5%

Government
12.4%

Buying and Selling to Businesses
5.7%

Transportation and Utilities (water, electricity, telephones) 7.6%

Buying and Selling to Consumers
9.9%

* Services include jobs in hotels, restaurants, auto repair, medicine, teaching, and entertainment.

Government

Montpelier is the capital of Vermont. The leaders of the state work in this city. Vermont's state government has three parts. They are the executive, legislative, and judicial branches.

Executive Branch

The job of the executive branch is to carry out the laws of the state. The governor leads the executive branch. The lieutenant governor helps the governor. A group of officials known as the cabinet also helps the governor.

Legislative Branch

The state legislature is called the General Assembly. It has two parts. They are the Senate and the House of Representatives.

The state capitol building is in Montpelier. It was built from granite mined near Barre.

Vermont legislators meet in the capitol building. Here, they are holding their first meeting of 2006.

These two groups work together to make laws for the state.

Judicial Branch

Judges and courts make up the judicial branch. Judges and courts may decide whether people who have been **accused of** committing crimes are guilty.

Local Government

Most cities are run by a mayor and council. Each town is led by a small group of people who are known as selectmen. They make daily decisions for the town. Every year in March, each town holds a town meeting. All of the town's **citizens** can attend. Together they decide on important issues that affect the whole town.

VERMONT'S STATE GOVERNMENT

Executive		Legislative		Judicial	
Office	**Length of Term**	**Body**	**Length of Term**	**Court**	**Length of Term**
Governor	2 years	Senate (30 members)	2 years	Supreme (5 justices)	6 years
Lieutenant Governor	2 years	House of Representatives (150 members)	2 years	Superior (15 judges)	6 years
				District Courts (17 judges)	6 years

Things to See and Do

If you are a skier or a snowboarder, you will like Vermont. Sometimes, people ski here for eight months of the year! The largest resort is Killington, which is not far from Rutland. Sugarbush and Stowe are two other popular ski areas.

Vermont offers other winter sports, too. Many state parks have beautiful cross-country ski trails. You can also go ice fishing and ice skating on lakes and ponds. And Stowe hosts a big winter carnival in January. It features an ice carving contest and just-for-fun events such as playing golf and volleyball in the snow. Winter is lots of fun in Vermont!

Skiers glide down a slope on Mount Mansfield.

Fun in Summer and Fall

Lake Champlain has crowds of visitors each summer. You can swim, canoe, kayak, and fish there. Vermont also has more than fifty state parks. Many of them offer hiking, camping, and water sports. You might want to go to Green Mountain National Forest, too. This is a great place to enjoy the wonders of nature.

In the fall, many people visit Vermont. Most come to see the colorful **foliage**. All over the state, tree leaves turn blazing gold, orange, and red. Mid-October is usually the best time to see fall color here.

Indoor Fun

Many of the cities and towns in Vermont have museums. One of them is in Shelburne. The Shelburne Museum has a great collection of old

The Green Mountain National Forest is in a beautiful part of the state. Here, a waterfall tumbles over rocks in a woodsy glen.

Famous People of Vermont

Jerry Greenfield

Born: March 14, 1951, Brooklyn, New York

Ben Cohen

Born: March 18, 1951, Brooklyn, New York

Jerry Greenfield and Ben Cohen have been friends since they were children. After they grew up, they learned how to make ice cream. The men moved to Vermont and opened an ice cream shop in Burlington. They created new flavor combinations and gave each flavor a funny name. Their ice creams became famous. Now, Ben & Jerry's ice cream is sold all over the country and has many fans.

If you go to Shelburne, be sure to visit the Shelburne Museum. There, you can explore this old steamboat from stem to stern.

barns, houses, and shops. They were moved here from other parts of the state. Now, you can walk through the buildings and see how people lived long ago. This museum has stagecoaches, old-time clothing and toys, and even a little circus carved out of wood.

Another place to visit is the Ethan Allen Homestead. This museum is in the city of Burlington. You can see Allen's last home and learn about his life and times.

If you like maple syrup, try to attend the Vermont Maple Festival. It is held in April in St. Albans. For maple treats, you can also go to St. Johnsbury. This town has a big factory that makes maple candy. Take a tour and sample some yummy maple products while you are there!

Long ago, some Vermont bridges were built with roofs. Today, you can still see many of these covered bridges around the state.

FUN FACTS

Sweet Treasure

Maple syrup has been made in Vermont for centuries. The Abenaki were making this sweet stuff long before the Europeans arrived. Maple sap is thin and has no color. It must be boiled down to make syrup. Forty gallons (151 liters) of sap are used to make 1 gallon (4 l) of syrup.

★ ★

accused of — blamed for

billboards — very large signs usually posted along roads and highways

century — a period of one hundred years, such as from 1900 through 1999

citizens — the people who live in a town, city, colony, or country

colonies — groups of people living in a new land but controlled by the place they came from

factories — buildings where products are made

foliage — leaves

immigrants — people who leave one country to live in another country

missionaries — people who travel to another land to teach other people about their religion

New England — a part of the northeastern United States made up of six states: Maine, Vermont, New Hampshire, Rhode Island, Massachusetts, and Connecticut

population — the number of people who live in a place such as a state

property — land

quarries — big pits where rock is mined for use in buildings

republic — a country that is run by a president who is elected by the people

resorts — vacation spots

thriving — healthy and growing

tourists — people who travel for fun

Union — the United States

Books

Ethan Allen. American War Biographies (series). Karen Price Hossell (Heinemann).

M is for Maple Syrup: A Vermont Alphabet. Discover America by State (series). Cynthia Furlong Reynolds (Sleeping Bear Press)

Vermont. This Land Is Your Land (series). Ann Heinrichs (Compass Point Books)

Vermont. United States (series). Paul Joseph (Abdo & Daughters)

Vermont Facts and Symbols. The States and Their Symbols (series). Kathy Feeney (Bridgestone Books)

Web Sites

Abenaki Indian Fact Sheet
www.geocities.com/bigorrin/abenaki_kids.htm

America's Story: Vermont Maple Syrup
www.americaslibrary.gov/cgi-bin/page.cgi/es/vt/syrup_1

Enchanted Learning: Vermont
www.enchantedlearning.com/usa/states/vermont/

Vermont Secretary of State's Kids' Page
www.sec.state.vt.us/kids/

Vermont State Parks: Just for Kids
www.vtstateparks.com/htm/kids.cfm

Abenaki people 6,7,16,29
African Americans 14
Allen, Ethan 4, 8, 29
Arthur, Chester A. 11, 13
Asian Americans 14

Barre 15, 17, 24
Brattleboro 7, 17
Burlington 5, 14, 15, 17, 18, 28, 29

Canada 6, 9, 10, 11, 15, 16
Champlain Canal 10
Champlain, Samuel de 6, 7, 13
Civil War, U.S. 11, 13
Clark, Kelly 27
Cohen, Ben 28
Colchester 5, 15
Connecticut River 18, 20, 21
Coolidge, Calvin 11, 13

education 16–17
Essex 5, 15

farming 9, 11, 12, 18, 22
Fort Dummer 7, 13
Fort Sainte Anne 7
France 6–7, 15

French and Indian War 7, 13

Garfield, James A. 11
granite 10, 11, 20, 23, 24
Great Britain 7–9, 10, 13, 15
Greenfield, Jerry 28
Green Mountain Boys 4, 8
Green Mountain National Forest 13, 27
Green Mountains 6, 7, 12, 18–20
Harding, Warren G. 11
Hispanics 14, 16
Hudson River 10

Ireland 10, 15
Iroquois people 6, 7
Italy 10, 15

Lake Champlain 6, 7, 10, 15, 18, 21, 27
lakes 21

maple syrup 9, 22, 29
marble 10, 20, 23
Montpelier 5, 15, 24
mountains 7, 20, 21
Mount Mansfield 20, 26

Native Americans 6, 14, 16

New Connecticut 9, 13
New Hampshire 7–9
New York 7–10
Northeast Highlands 20

Paterson, Katherine 17
Powers, Ross 27

railroads 10, 15
religion 16
Revolutionary War 8, 9
rivers 20–21
Rutland 5, 15, 26

St. Albans 11, 22, 29
Shelburne 27, 28
slavery 9
snowboarding 26, 27

Taconic Mountains 18, 20
tourism 11, 12, 23, 27

Vergennes 10, 13
Vermont Valley 18
voting rights 9

Wales 10, 15
War of 1812 10, 13
Winter Olympic Games 27

World War I 11, 13
World War II 11, 13